PILGRIM

PURSUIT OF APPINESS

First Printing: July 2013 V2

ISBN: 978-1-937735-55-5

Legends Library Publishing Inc. Honeoye Falls, New York

Send publishing inquiries to: info@legendslibrary.com
or visit www.legendslibrary.org

Book interior layout and cover design by Alisha Bishop

To reach Leo and Nancy Martin or Jenney House tours, visit:

www.thejenney.org

Or send email to: nancy@thejenney.org or leo@thejenney.org

PILGRIM
PURSUIT OF *Happiness*

LEO MARTIN

Foreword by Dr. Paul Jehle

New York

Monument to the Forefathers in Plymouth, MA

Dedicated 1889

CONTENTS

Foreword .... *i*

Preface.. *iii*

Acknowledgements .... *v*

Dedication .... *vii*

Chapter One..1
    Spiritual Liberty

Chapter Two..7
    Religious Liberty

Chapter Three 13
    Political Liberty

Chapter Four...21
    Constitutional Liberty

Chapter Five..35
    Economic Liberty

Chapter Six...45
    Prayer

Epilogue...49

Bibliography...53

About the Author 55

About the Jenney Museum 57

Publisher Note...59

FOREWORD

The Declaration of Independence states that one of our unalienable rights is the *pursuit of happiness.* It is clear from the records of both Virginia and Massachusetts at the time that this phrase meant the right to privately own property. However, what is also clear is that the unalienable right we have is to *pursue* happiness and not *obtain happiness.* Today Americans often mistake the meaning of this phrase and think that their government owes them happiness in all flavors, to be claimed by them at any time. What Leo Martin has done is to clearly articulate the meaning of this phrase by going to the root of our country, the Pilgrims. No other people at the time of our nation's initial development portray, as families and a migrating Church, the meaning of *pursuing* happiness under the Hand of a Sovereign God better than this tiny band.

Though never in a majority and never wealthy; they considered themselves to be rich in spiritual treasure. Though they sought no shrine to honor themselves, a nation has honored them as the root of its liberty though in our day they have been largely forgotten. It is time we returned to what truly made

America great. It is time we remembered the nature of the liberties brought by the Pilgrims in their simple faith, heart-felt devotion and iron-clad character. Though the seeds planted by them eventually grew into a tree much larger and with leaves a bit different in color than they may have anticipated, their love of family, their stand for freedom, and their faith in God stand tall and point in the direction toward which our nation can recover from her amnesia. Let this little book be read and re-read to your children and grandchildren, that the stories of our past may come alive again.

—Dr. Paul Jehle

Executive Director -Plymouth Rock Foundation

PREFACE

 W hat were our Pilgrims all about and what kind of legacy did they leave our country. Their story is far reaching. To understand their journey we should begin by looking at the labels assigned them along the way. William Bradford referred to our travelers as "Pilgrims" just one time in his book, *Of Plymouth Plantation*, and the name stuck because they were on a religious journey, or pilgrimage, which earned them this name.

When they left the Church of England, they were labeled "Separatists." The Separatists shared the Mayflower with another group of people who left for other reasons. To distinguish between the two groups the "Separatists" were now called the "Saints" and the other group the "Strangers." When they made the deal to finance the voyage, they were to travel to the New World and begin a Plantation that would produce a profit for the people financing the trip. From a business point of view they were now called "Planters," and the people doing the financing were called the "Adventurers." Most historians, however, refer to the Pilgrims as the "Forefathers," the people who came to the New Word to set in motion the liberties we find in our country today. In Plymouth, we honor the Pilgrims with the

Forefathers Monument that tells the story of a people of faith and courage upon which our nation was founded on. Here is that story.

ACKNOWLEDGEMENTS

I would like to thank Dr. Paul Jehle, of Plymouth Rock Foundation for sharing his vast knowledge of the Pilgrims with me. I could not have completed this book without his guidance and direction. Thank you to Mrs. Pat Clark who spent endless hours editing the story making sure that the thought process flowed. And thank you especially to my wife Nancy who pushed me to complete the project and kept me on track. I love you.

DEDICATION

This book is dedicated to Dr. Charles Wolf of Plymouth Rock Foundation for his devotion to the Pilgrim story and for his dedication to keep the story alive.

The Declaration of Independence declares that all men are created equal, that they are endowed by their Creator with certain unalienable rights, that among these are Life, Liberty and the pursuit of Happiness ... not the right to happiness but the right to the pursuit of happiness. Was the Pilgrim journey motivated by their pursuit of happiness and if so, in the midst of their suffering and setbacks, did they achieve it ... and most importantly what, to them, was happiness?

CHAPTER ONE

Spiritual Liberty

Who were these Pilgrims, or Forefathers, where did they come from and why did they take this pilgrimage? The answer begins with their leader and pastor, John Robinson. John Robinson was the driving force behind the Pilgrim movement. He was a graduate of Corpus Christi College and was considered one of the top theologians of his time. He exhibited a great humanity as a pastor and demonstrated an incredible tolerance in a very intolerant age. We will see these attributes reflected throughout the pilgrimage our Forefathers took in the flight from Europe to Plymouth. John Robinson was a product of the reformation and one of the foremost supporters of Puritan thought.

At this time an excellent and relatively inexpensive Bible was being printed. It listed chapter and verses making it easy to read; it contained many footnotes making it a useful study Bible. This Geneva Bible helped the Pilgrims to live out their belief built upon the foundation laid by Luther, Calvin, and others, that they no longer needed a bishop, king, or priest to intercede between them and God. They could understand God directly by reading God's Word; by praying they could talk directly to God. Through that, they felt God talked back to them. They had a two-way conversation with God! They went from having someone intercede between them and God to talking personally to God, which resulted in a relationship with God. They now had a different faith because they had a personal relationship with God and this changed them on the inside.

Pilgrims going to church

At this time, King James was the King of England and the head of the Anglican Church and as such, he made the law in England for everyone. Everyone was under the same rule of law in England, except King James.

He was above the law. He did not have to follow his own law. If you wanted to pray in England, you could pray all day long, as long as the subject of your prayer was King James. King James thought he was God! He stated, "The state of monarchy is the supremest thing on earth; for Kings are not only God's lieutenants upon earth and sit on God's throne, but even by God Himself they are called gods. King James called this the "divine right of the King" and it did not sit well with John Robinson so he removed his people from the Anglican Church and they began to have church in their homes. In other words, they separated from the Anglican Church. That is why the Pilgrims are called Separatists.

King James

The Puritans were theologically very similar to the Separatists but they stayed in the Anglican Church and tried to purify it from within. That is why they are called Puritans making this one of the major differences between the Puritans and Pastor Robinson and the Separatists. Not only did the faith of the Pilgrims change, their moral standard changed. It changed from the moral standard of King James to the moral standard of God. Faith and morality are inward governances. When these change, you are different on the inside. You now have a faith in God, not man, and your moral standard is based on the truth of the Bible not on the laws of man. The Pilgrims were no longer told how to worship or who to worship. They had a direct line to God, their King...King Jesus. They now had Spiritual Liberty.

"When as by the travail and diligence of some godly and zealous preachers, and God's blessing on their labors, as in other places of the land, so in the north parts, many became enlightened by the Word of God and had their ignorance and sins discovered unto them, and began by His grace to reform their lives and make conscience of their ways."

—Governor William Bradford

Statue of Faith

William Bradford

CHAPTER TWO

Religious Liberty

Austerfield, England

William Bradford lost his parents as a young boy, and his uncle in Austerfield England raised him. As a teen-ager, he would walk many miles from Austerfield to Scrooby England in order to attend the Pilgrim Church there. He valued this Bible teaching and fellowship and this Spiritual Liberty. His uncle did not approve of Bradford going to this church and disowned him because of this practice. William Bradford, however, valued his church so highly that even his family could not stop him from going to the church at the home of William Brewster even though it was outlawed by King James. Most of the people in Scrooby valued this fellowship as much as Bradford and it became noticeable that the people of Scrooby were not going to the church run by King James. It was also well known that these people worshiped God and that they must be gathering somewhere. The King wanted to find out where and put an end to the practice.

Scrooby Manor

On the Sabbath, men were sent by the King to watch the Separatists at Scrooby to see where they might be meeting. They noticed that they were going into William Brewster's house and reported to the King that they must be going there to worship. A little later, some strangers came into the house and delivered a message to Pastor John Robinson, and then left. The message was from King James and it ordered the Separatists to go to his church and worship according to the laws of England, or not to worship at all. They were determined to keep their Spiritual Liberty and not go to the Church of England. They began to change the locations of their meetings from home to home, so they would not be stopped from worshiping together. They would even worship at night, in the dark, so they would not be found out. However, King James kept sending spies to watch this congregation until they were caught worshiping together again. The men were arrested and the women and children were sent back to their lonely homes. After a time the men were released from prison. During this time, William Bradford said that church members:

"Were hunted and persecuted on every side, so as their former afflictions were as flea bitings in comparison with these that now came upon them. For some were taken and clapt up in prison, others had their houses beset and watcht night and day, and hardly escaped their hands; and most were faine to flie and leave their howses and habitations, and the means of their livelihood."

They needed to make a decision. Should they continue to meet secretly or should they go back to the King's Church. They were not willing to give up the Spiritual Liberty they found in their relationship with God, but if the persecution continued, they would not have the Religious Liberty they needed to follow this path. In 1607, they decided to move to Holland where the government allowed religious freedom. Because King James did not want the Pilgrims escaping to Holland, he continued to arrest some, like William Brewster. It took them a year, with much hardship and great financial cost, to complete the move. They moved to Amsterdam but found conflict with other English churches so they removed themselves to Leiden where they built their community. John Robinson would be their pastor and William Brewster would be the ruling elder. In the church they built there, they would continue their Spiritual Liberty and finally achieve the Religious Liberty for which they were searching.

"Yet seeing themselves thus molested, and there was no hope of their continuance there, by a joint consent they resolved to go into the Low Countries, where they herd was freedom of religion for all men..."

—Governor William Bradford

Holland

CHAPTER THREE

Political Liberty

Leiden Holland was a much different place then Scrooby England. The houses were brightly colored, with very steep roofs. Some of the houses were tilted to one side because they were built on long posts that sank into the soft ground; over time these would settle at different levels. The Hollanders had to build large dikes to keep out the sea, and everywhere there were windmills that looked like giants, grinding grain and pumping water from the land. There were canals that ran through the town like roads with canal boats traveling up and down carrying goods.

Edward Winslow

Things were also different for the men of Scrooby. Because they were poor and unable to buy land to build farms, they had to search for other ways to earn a living. John Robinson studied and taught at Leiden University; William Brewster,

13

with the help of Edward Winslow, became a book publisher. Most of the congregation worked in the clothing trade to support themselves. Some were tailors, fustian makers, hat makers, and wool carders; others worked in the weaving, dying, and sewing trades. The work was hard, and they worked long hours to survive and to try to save a little money. They honored their employers and earned a reputation as hard workers and honest men, even to the point that they would be hired before the local people. Still they were foreigners, employment opportunities were few, and the long hours of work barely kept up their poor standard of living.

Dutch church in Leiden

Their church in Leiden was in Pastor John Robinson's large house, and they no longer had to worry about being found out. They had Religious Liberty. Near the pastor's house was one of the largest churches in Leiden. As the Pilgrims walked to their Sunday service, they would pass many Hollanders on their way to church. The Pilgrims could hear them as they walked by in their carved wooden shoes, dressed in their best suits and colorful dresses. The Pilgrims assembled in their plain suits and dresses and simple hats—all they had to wear. Yet, when they met the Hollanders, the Pilgrims greeted them happily, and in their church service, they sang with joy, knowing they would no longer be persecuted for their beliefs.

As the years passed, they found that Holland was a hard country, and very few of their friends in England wanted to join them. The hard work was taking its toll. They were growing old before their time, and their children were feeling the same effects. Out of necessity, the children worked at the same hard jobs for the same long hours and were suffering ill health in their early youth. The babies born in Holland grew up learning the Dutch language as easily as English. In some cases, they preferred it.

The children liked the brightly colored clothes and the wooden shoes, and they began to assimilate into the Dutch way of life. This distressed the Pilgrim parents. They wanted their children to remember the English language and the English way of life. The men wanted to own farms where they and their sons could work the earth with their own hands. They wanted their children to remember why they came to Holland in the first place. They wanted the next generation to embrace Spiritual and Religious Liberty and to build their lives based on the Bible. They also wanted to advance the Kingdom of God in the remote parts of the Earth.

They needed to move again to a place where they could build a society based on Biblical principles, where they could have Spiritual and Religious Liberty, and where they could build a political system that would honor God and not man. In the "dominion charter" in

Genesis (1: 26-28) we are told to take dominion over the earth. We are made in God's image and are to rule over the fish and the birds and the cattle and things that creep and crawl on the earth, but not over each other. The Pilgrims believed that the only one to rule over people made in God's image was King Jesus.

We are all equal in God's sight. God honors the individual, and if God honors the individual, we should too. The Pilgrims wanted to build a political system where all people were equal under the law— not equal in gifts and abilities, but equal under the law. When Pastor Robinson removed himself and his congregation from the church of King James to start the journey towards Spiritual Liberty, he did not want to see one person in charge of everything, so he asked his congregation to elect him pastor, not to appoint him. An elected leader can be unelected. There would be no "king" with absolute rule. This idea would eventually change the political system by removing the power of the king and giving the power to the individual. They would now begin to decentralize the government by granting to the people the power to choose their leaders and their laws.

Since the Pilgrims had achieved Spiritual Liberty, and their faith and morality had changed, their inward governance had also changed. Because they had achieved a new spiritual level, they were able to practice self-government. As they changed on the inside, this transition was reflected on the outside. The Pilgrim's early experience with self-government became a building block for a representative republic where people elect representatives who are responsible to the people, and who can be voted out by the people. However, this system requires responsibility of the voters to put people in office who have excellent character, integrity, and moral standards. Many years later, John Adams said, *"Our Constitution was made only for a moral and religious people. It is wholly inadequate to the government of any other."*

To fulfill "Dominion Charter" and the Great Commission (to go and make disciples of all nations) the Pilgrims put plans in motion to cross a vast ocean. They would set up a political system based on the voluntary choice of self-rule resulting in Political Liberty. After almost twelve years in Holland, they sailed for the New World.

"So they left that goodly and pleasant city which had been their resting place near twelve years; but they knew they were pilgrims and looked not much on those things, but lift up their eyes to the heavens, their dearest country, and quieted their spirits."

—Governor William Bradford

CHAPTER FOUR

Constitutional Liberty

Once the Pilgrims had decided to leave, the choice of where to settle needed to be made. After humble prayers to God asking for His protection and assistance, the men had a conference to decide upon their destination. Some favored Guiana with its fertile soil and warm climate; others preferred Virginia where the English had already begun to settle. Those who were opposed to Guiana felt that even though the country was warm and pleasant and had rich soil that would produce much, it would not be the right place for them. Their bodies, accustomed to cooler climates, would be inclined to fall prey to the diseases and heat of Guiana. In addition, there was danger that the Spanish in that area would harass and try to drive them away. The objection to Virginia was that if they settled there, the Pilgrims would have to live under the rule of the existing colony and would be in danger of being persecuted for their religious beliefs, just as if they still lived in England.

Jamestown

After long discussion, they concluded that they should live as a separate body under the general government of Virginia. Therefore, they sent two of their congregation to England to obtain a patent (a kind of license) granting them freedom to settle in the Virginia territory, but as far away as possible from the existing colony at Jamestown. When the patent was presented to the king for his approval, he said he would not stop them as long as they caused no trouble. To the king, the Pilgrims had become an annoyance, and he just wanted them to go away. However, to publicly allow their claim to religious freedom, under the King's seal, was out of the question. Some felt that it was dangerous to go without assurance of religious freedom, as they would not be building this move on a solid foundation. On the other hand, even if they had the kings blessing, he could remove his seal any time. The elders felt that they should

22

trust God's providence for the outcome and that they should proceed. Their representatives were to secure the patent and find merchants and other interested parties to help finance the voyage.

Embarkation

Thomas Weston, a London merchant, was contracted to pull together the interested parties and to work on the terms of the financial agreement. The Pilgrims' representatives, John Carver and Robert Cushman, were admonished not to exceed the bounds of their commission in their eagerness to find investors. In order to repay the debts they were incurring, the colonists sought a deal whereby they would work four days a week for the investors and two days a week on their own "particular" plots to avoid being merely servants. In addition, at the end of seven years they would own their own land and not have to split it with the investors. This agreement was sent back to Leiden for approval. The Pilgrims were encouraged to move quickly and to be ready to leave as soon as possible. They sold their possessions and prepared for the trip. Then they received notice that Thomas Weston had changed the agreement. The Pilgrims would work six of six days for the common store and at the end of seven years, everything would be divided equally between the investors and the colonists. With the travelers' property sold and everyone ready to go, Cushman felt he had no choice but to accept the agreement. He did exactly what he was asked not to do and exceeded his commission to satisfy the financers. The Pilgrims had to take the agreement and proceed.

The Pilgrims bought a boat called the Speedwell that took them from Holland to England to meet the Mayflower, which they leased. The two ships were to make the trip to Northern Virginia together. Not all the people on the Mayflower were Pilgrims, or Separatists. Besides the crews, there were those coming for financial reasons and those wanting a new start in life. About half their numbers were Pilgrims, or "Saints" as they called themselves, and the other half were referred to as "Strangers"—meaning "strangers to the faith."

They set sail from England, but as they traveled, the Speedwell began to leak and they had to return twice for repair. Finally, it was decided that the Speedwell could not be repaired; it was sold for half of what they had paid for it. About twenty of the travelers had to stay behind because there was not enough room on the Mayflower. Because the seas had been very rough during the first two attempts to leave, some of the passengers were happy to volunteer to remain behind, but not William Bradford. Determined and focused on God, Bradford said,

"And thus, like Gideon's army, this small number was divided, as if the Lord by this work of His providence thought these few too many for the great work he had to do."

Praying on the Speedwell

Mayflower

The journey finally began and lasted sixty-six days. During the trip, only two people died on the Mayflower, one sailor and one Pilgrim. The Pilgrim was a man named William Button, a servant to the doctor, Samuel Fuller. Button's job was to give a lemon or a lime to each person to prevent them from getting scurvy. Because he did not like the taste, Button did not take them himself, and he died of the disease. The sailor who died was the bosun's mate who hated the Pilgrims. Because of the rough crossing, the Pilgrims were sick for much of the trip, but they would still stand in the hold of the ship praying and singing hymns. This so annoyed the bosun's mate that he exclaimed, "I cannot wait until you people die and I can put your bodies in a shroud and dump you into the ocean you hymn singing puke stockings!" The next week, he was the one who died, and it was the Pilgrims who put *his* body in a shroud and dumped *him* into the ocean. To this day, we do not know how he died, but not another sailor had a word to say against the Pilgrims for the rest of the trip.

Two babies were born on the voyage. Oceanus Hopkins was born half-way across the ocean so they named him Oceanus; Peregrine White was born in Provincetown Harbor. Peregrine means little wanderer or little pilgrim. One Pilgrim fell overboard during the trip; he was John Howland, a servant to John Carver. About half way through the trip, he needed some fresh air, went up on the deck, and was swept into the ocean by a wave. As he went in, he grabbed a rope from the ship that was hanging over the side. The sailors were able to pull him back on board, thus saving his life. John Howland went on to produce the largest number of Mayflower descendants in the country. Included among them are Presidents George and George W Bush, Franklin D. Roosevelt, and Sir Winston Churchill.

Because of the rough crossing and strong winds, the Mayflower was blown off course about two hundred miles, landing on Cape Cod instead of the Hudson River area where they were planning to go. All of this area was at the time considered part of Northern Virginia. They tried to correct their error by going out around the tip of Cape Cod, but because of the lateness of the season, (late November) the ocean was too rough to pass, so they stayed in what is now called Provincetown Harbor. Only some weeks later would they move the ship to Plymouth.

John Howlans falling off the Mayflower

Landing on Provincetown Harbor

The patent they were given was for Northern Virginia, not for Cape Cod, so there was no law to govern or keep them there. Because of this, the Strangers did not want to sit under the rule of the Saints. The Strangers threatened to leave and form their own settlement elsewhere. This gave the Pilgrims the first opportunity to exercise their Political Liberty outside the church. They decided to take a vote of all adult males (well enough to sin) on board in order to elect a leader and to agree on rules to govern the group. Once the leader was elected, all would follow him, whether they voted for him or not. John Carver was unanimously elected the first governor of Plymouth Colony, and self-rule in this country began. The Pilgrims wrote down their agreement so there would be no question as to what they agreed to. This document is called the Mayflower Compact. All 41 of the men signed it—the first document of self-rule in our country, and the beginning of Constitutional Liberty.

Signing the Mayflower Compact

The Mayflower Compact - November 11, 1620

In y^e name of God Amen· We whose names are vnderwriten, the loyall subjects of our dread soveraigne Lord King James by y^e grace of God, of great Britaine, franc, & Ireland king, defender of ye faith, &c Haveing vndertaken, for ye glorie of God, and advancemente of ye christian ^faith and honour of our king & countrie, a voyage to plant ye first colonie in ye Northerne parts of Virginia· doe by these presents solemnly & mutualy in ye presence of God, and one of another, covenant, & combine our selves togeather into a civill body politick; for ye our better ordering, & preservation & furtherance of ye ends aforesaid; and by vertue hearof, to *enacte, constitute, and frame shuch just & equall lawes, ordinances, Acts, constitutions, & offices, from time to time, as shall be thought most meete & convenient for yᵉ generall good of yᵉ colonie: vnto which we promise all due submission and obedience. In witnes wherof we have herevnder subscribed our names at Cap Codd yᵉ ·11· of November, in yᵉ year of yᵉ raigne of our soveraigne Lord king James of England, france, & Ireland yᵉ eighteenth and of Scotland yᵉ fiftie fourth. Anᵒ: Dom ·1620·*

The Mayflower Compact was a covenant promise under God to first honor God, then the people, and lastly the king. The Compact marked the beginning of our American Republic. It may be considered the Pilgrims "Declaration of Independence," establishing a civil self-government promising to enact just and equal laws. Even though the Mayflower Compact was signed by 41 male adults and it was unanimous, it was not officially recognized by the English authorities. In 1621 the Pierce Patent was sent and was recognized by the king. For the Pilgrims the Pierce Patent was a secular law that represented the rule of the king ruling from the top down. According to the Mayflower Compact the people ruled and honored God. The Pilgrims functioned by this act of self-government, and the Compact was repeated as a "preamble" to every subsequent edition of their laws for decades.

The Pilgrims felt that if they treated each other justly and equally, they should treat other people in the same way. In 1621, they signed a peace treaty with the Indians that lasted fifty-five years, the longest lasting peace treaty in the history of our country. This document was written down so both parties could understand it. But how were they able to understand each other so well when they did not speak the same language? Several years earlier some hunters and fishermen came to trade with the Indians. One man, named Hunt, invited an Indian aboard his ship to trade, then captured him, and took him back to England as a slave. He was named Squanto. While in England Squanto learned English, attained his freedom, and returned to Plymouth about six months before the Pilgrims arrived. Squanto lived with the Pilgrims and became their interpreter and advisor. Governor Bradford called Squanto his special gift from God.

Peace Treaty

Peace Treaty – March 21, 1621

1. That neither he nor any of his should injure or do hurt to any of our people.

2. And if any of his did do hurt to any of ours, he should send the offender, that we might punish him.

3. That if any of our tools were taken away when our people were at work, he should cause them to be restored, and if ours did any harm to any of his, we would do the like to them.

4. If any did unjustly war against him, we would aid him; if any did war against us, he should aid us.

5. He should send to his neighbor confederates, to certify them of this, that they might not wrong us, but might be likewise comprised in the conditions of peace.

6. That when their men came to us, they should leave their bows and arrows behind them, as we should do our pieces when we came to them.

7. Lastly, that doing thus, King James would esteem of him as his friend and ally.

From 1636 to 1671, the Plymouth Colonists formulated a series of laws which they later compiled into a declaration called "The General Fundamentals." This declaration has often been viewed by historians as one of the earliest demands for representative government and individual rights in the American Colonies. They achieved Constitutional Liberty with written declarations of their Political Liberty, which helped them for a civil body politic.

"Occasioned partly by the discontented and mutinous speeches that some of the strangers amongst them had let fall from them in the ship; that when they came ashore they would use their own liberty, for none had the power to command them, the patent they had being for Virginia and not for New England... and partly that such an act by them done, this their condition considered, might be as firm as any patent, and in some respects more sure."

—**Governor William Bradford**

CHAPTER FIVE

Economic Liberty

The Pilgrims Economic and Constitutional Liberties made everyone equal under the law. To be equal under the law gives individuals equal say in who governs them, which gives more value to each individual in a civil government. People, however, do not have equal gifts and talents, drive or focus. We are all made differently. In a righteous civil government, the individual must be given the freedom to exercise their gifts and reap the benefits of both their giftedness and ambition. There is a great kinship between a righteous civil government and a righteous economy.

As Miss Verna M. Hall put it, "Government is the house in which the economy lives." Under the agreement made between Thomas Weston and the Pilgrims, everyone was the "same." All would be equally rewarded regardless of talent or ambition. The principle of civil self-government and the economic success ran counter to what the financers demanded, and eventually an adjustment would have to be necessary. When the Pilgrims originally came to Plymouth they were forced into a communal existence by their contract with Thomas Weston and the financers of the trip. They were all required to work a common field, put everything into a common store, and dole out evenly what they needed to survive. The rest would go to the financers. Any profits made from logging, fishing, or trade would also used to pay off their debt. The financers, also called the Adventurers, and the Pilgrims, called Planters or the Workers had a very one-side arrangement. It recognized the right of the Adventurers to a profit, but did not recognize the rights of those who were Planters. William Bradford describes this in his diary, *Of Plimouth Plantation;*

> *The chief and principal differences between these and the former conditions, stood in those two points; that the houses, and lands improved, especially gardens and home lots, should remain undivided wholly to the planters at the seven years' end. Secondly, that they should have had two days in a week for their own private employment, for the more comfort of themselves and their families, especially such as had families.*

Of the one hundred and two passengers on the Mayflower, fifty-one died the first winter, and even more died within the first three years. Some died of disease and some of starvation because they did not produce enough food. There was not enough incentive for everyone to work hard. However, from 1623 on they had a great improvement in their lives because William Bradford changed the way they did business. From then on, every family had their own land, planted their own food, and then traded with each other to meet their needs. Unmarried adults either worked their own land, or more likely, were assigned to families who needed an extra hand. This worked so well that they never had a starving day after that, and they tripled their production. This left the problem of how to divide the land. The Pilgrims divided their land according to the number of people in each family. If you produced more children, you would have more land, which would encourage larger families. Since they had only fifty-one people, they needed to increase the population, and it worked. Today, around ten percent of the population of the United States are Mayflower descendants.... thirty million people from fifty-one.

"This had good success, for it made all hands industrious, so as much more corn was planted than otherwise might have been by any means the Governor or any other could use, and saved him a great deal of trouble, and gave far better content. The women now went willingly into the field, and took their little ones with them to set corn; which before would allege weakness and inability; whom to have

compelled *would have been thought great tyranny and oppression."*

—**Governor William Bradford**

Bradford's "ingredients" for a Free Economy

Bradford identifies several reasons why socialism (common ownership of labor) and elementary communism (common ownership of land) did not work, even among the most godly people. We can deduce at least the following from his discourse describing their 1623 decision.

1. In a common ownership of labor and land, people tend to become lazy, not wanting to work, thus *private property* must undergird a free and productive economy.

2. Under socialism, people tend to make up excuses why they can't work, thus *private profit* is a key ingredient in a free economy as well.

3. Communal living breeds discontent, for all tend to want what others have, but refuse to work for it, thus *welfare must be voluntary (private charity) rather than forced (government charity)*.

4. Socialism is built on pride and a presumed external equality in an open or ignorant refusal of God's plan in the Bible so that differences between the young, adult or aged are not respected. *A free economy is built, in contrast, on the respect and dignity of individual differences.*

5. Though some look at the profit motive as corrupt, it is imperative to see that it is man's nature that is corrupt, including those who hold office in government. *The free market, in contrast, is built on personal incentive and self-interest in order to overcome one's naturally corrupt nature..*

6. Ultimately, God's design for the economy rests on *voluntary choice*, which is far more productive than government force and the re-distribution of wealth.

Trading Post

The Adventurers and Planters had entered into a business arrangement that had risk on both sides. The Planters risked their very lives by making this trip, and the Adventurers risked their investment. Despite stacking the deck heavily in their favor, the Adventurers had simply made an unprofitable investment. From a strictly business view -point, the Planters did not have a "debt" at all. However, they displayed a high level of Christian character by paying off their "debt," recognizing that the private profit system made the expedition possible, since it provided the only practical way to finance the voyage. The Adventurers were also responsible for sending more supplies as needed to support the Plantation. They did not fulfill this obligation, leaving the Pilgrims to fend for themselves with no outside support. This made

Plimouth Plantation the first self-sustaining colony. They had to use what resources they had to survive and prosper. They felt that each person should seek the gifts or talents that God had given them and use them for the good of the colony. Each should find a product or service he could produce best, and then freely and openly exchange the fruits of his labors with others in a free market. This is the outworking of voluntary political and economic union.

Grist Mill

While most of the Pilgrims were Planters, not all grew crops. Some hunted and fished, some were carpenters or made clothes, and others devoted themselves to trade. In 1627, the Pilgrims built a trading post at Aptuxcet in a town now called Bourne. The river on which it was located has since been transformed into the Cape Cod Canal. At this trading post, the Pilgrims engaged in a three-way trading system. This was a free and peaceful trade, without tariffs, among the Pilgrims, the Dutchmen from New Netherlands (New York), and the Indians from Rhode Island and Cape Cod. This free market allowed all to benefit from the productive talents God had given to each individual.

One of the things that separate men from all the animals is that he was given the creative intelligence that allows him to create tools. These tools would make him more productive and allow him to produce things with great precision. In 1636, John Jenney finished building a gristmill on Town Brook at Plimouth Plantation. For their first sixteen years in Plymouth, the Pilgrims pounded their corn in mortars. This time consuming process did not satisfy the needs of a growing population. To satisfy that need, John Jenney built a grinding mill that would vastly increase production. To do this John Jenney would not be able to go out in the field and produce for himself anymore, which resulted in him having to be paid for his services. He was then able to reinvest his profits, which allowed him to build a brewery and a bakery and resulted in his becoming a wealthy businessman. This once again demonstrated the fruitful results of a free market. The kinship between a righteous civil government and a righteous economy was now complete *resulting in Economic Liberty.*

"The experience that was had in this common course and condition, tried sundry years and that amongst godly and sober men, may well evince the vanity of that conceit of Plato's and other ancients applauded by some of later times; that the taking away of property and bringing in community into a commonwealth would make them happy and flourishing; as if they were wise than God."

—Governor William Bradford

CHAPTER SIX

Prayer

As we have seen over the course of this pilgrimage, the five liberties the Pilgrims were pursuing were intertwined. The one thread running through all the liberties, and holding them together, was prayer.

When they formed their first Church in England, they made a covenant together to beseech God in prayer and met in Scrooby Manor for that purpose. The decision to leave England was made only after asking God, in prayer, for guidance. When the Pilgrims boarded the Speedwell, John Robinson led them in prayer asking that they would keep their focus on God and do His Will. Upon landing on the tip of Cape Cod at Provencetown, they blessed the God of Heaven for delivering them back to dry land. Even though half their number had died, when they had an "adequate" harvest, Governor Bradford called for a celebration to thank God for his blessings. This is considered the first Thanksgiving that gave birth to our Thanksgiving tradition today.

The Pilgrims accomplished a lot when they put God first and glorified him in what they did. When they changed from a socialistic economic system to a capitalist system, tripling their production, they were confident that their starving time was over. They felt that their economic system was good and just.

But after all they had been through and finally figuring out how to produce more, they were faced with a new challange. There was a servere drought on Plimouth Plantation and on Hobomock's village, their close Indian neighbors just across the river. The drought lasted for two months, and all their crops wilted. Again they turned to God. On a Wednesday morning in July, William Bradford called for a day of prayer and humiliation to ask God what they had done wrong. When they began to pray there was not a cloud in the sky, but by the afternoon it began to cloud up, and by evening it began to rain. Not the hard rain, that they were used to, but a soft gentle rain. It fell for two weeks, on both villages, and the crops were saved. When Hobomock saw what the Pilgrim's God could do, he became a Christian. The problem was not that they turned *to* God, but that they turned *back to* God. They may well have wanted to take credit for their economic success, thinking it was *their* idea, not *God's*. This incident may have shown them that they could never forget their reliance on the Providence of God. I believe that if you could ask a Pilgrim about their economy, they might just tell you, "it's not *our* economy at all, it's God's. All we need to do is follow Him."

"Being thus constrained to leave their native soil and country, their lands and livings, and all their friends

and familiar acquaintance, it was much; and thought marvelous to many....it was by many thought an adventure almost desperate; a case intolerable and a misery worse than death.... But these things did not dismay them, though they did sometimes trouble them; for their desires were set on the ways of God and to enjoy His ordinances; but they rested on His providence, and knew Whom they had believed."

—**Governor William Bradford**

Epilogue

This pilgrimage of a few English Pilgrims was not a casual strole through life. It was a directional journey in which the Pilgrims sought the Will of God in their lives. And at their journey's end, I believe they would feel able to stand before God and hear Him say, "Well done my good and faithful servant."

The Pilgrims, our Forefathers, also left a legacy to our founding fathers and to us all—a legacy of these five liberties on which the founding of our country rests. They were used by the authors of the Declaration of Independence and of the Constitution to help guide their decisions and to strengthen their resolve in establishing a new nation. Our country is a Christian country built on Judeo-Christian principles, and this is a good thing. Christianity is inclusive. You do not need to be a Christian to reap the benefits of a Christian nation. God does not say all *Christians* are equal under the law, but that all *people* are equal under the law. Let us resolve to remember their legacy and to continue their pilgimage.

"And for the support of this Declaration, with a firm reliance on the protection of Divine Providence, we mutually pledge to each other our Lives, our Fortunes and our sacred Honor."

—The Declaration of Independence

THUS OUT OF SMALL
BEGINNINGS GREATER THINGS
HAVE BEEN PRODUCED BY HIS
HAND THAT MADE ALL THINGS
OF NOTHING, AND GIVES BEING
TO ALL THINGS THAT ARE.
AND AS ONE SMALL CANDLE
MAY LIGHT A THOUSAND, SO
THE LIGHT HERE KINDLED
HATH SHONE UNTO MANY, YEA
IN SOME SORT TO OUR WHOLE
NATION: LET THE GLORIOUS
NAME OF JEHOVAH HAVE ALL
THE PRAISE.

GOVERNOR WILLIAM BRADFORD

BIBLIOGRAPHY

Wolfe, Charles, *Who Were the Pilgrims?* Plymouth Rock Foundation Newsletter, Volume 25, Issue 5, September/October, 2002

Wolfe, Charles, *Economic Principles of the Pilgrims*

Wolfe, Charles, *America's First Economist*

Bartlett, Robert M., *The Pilgrim Way*

Jehle, Dr. Paul, *Legacy of the Pilgrims*

Hall, Verna, *The Christian History of the Constitution of the United States of America: Christian Self-Government*

Slater, Rosalie, *Teaching and Learning America's Christian History: The Principal Approach*

Rose, James B. , *A Guide to American Christian Education for the Home and School: The Principal Approach*

Bethell, Tom, *How Private Property Saved the Pilgrims*

Patton, Dr. Judd W., *The Pilgrim Story: Vital Insights and Lessons for Today*

Hosmer, William M., *Pilgrims Free Themselves from Communism: Establish Individual Enterprise*

North, Greg, *Puritan Economic Experiments*

Kuyper, Abraham, *Christianity; A Total World and Life System*

Stratton, Eugene Aubrey, *Plymouth Colony Its History and People 1620-1691*

Paget, Harold, *Of Plymouth Plantation*

Fiore, Jordan, ed., *Mourt's Relation, A Journal of the Pilgrim's of Plymouth., first published in 1622, republished by the Plymouth Rock Foundation, 1985*

ABOUT THE AUTHOR

Leo Martin, an educator and expert on the early history of our nation, has been called "the last God-fearing guide in historic Plymouth, MA." While so many others are taking God out of the history books, Martin maintains that the Pilgrims and Founding Fathers established "one nation under God," founded on Judeo-Christian values. A true patriot and historian, Leo Martin is the Education Director at the Jenney Museum in Plymouth, MA, where he is known for his service giving historical tours and lectures dressed in Pilgrim costume. He is a champion of our nation's founding values displayed in the National Monument to the Forefathers in Plymouth. Director of Destination Plymouth. Leo has been married to his wife, Nancy, since 1973. They have been working together in Plymouth giving historic tours since 2001. They have three children and four grandchildren.

ABOUT THE JENNEY

Founded in 2004 by Leo and Nancy Martin, the Jenney is dedicated to conveying the impact 51 Pilgrims had on the founding and ongoing development of the United States and the the importance of passing on the history of our country from generation to generation.

The Jenney offers tours of the historic district of Plymouth and the National Monument to the Forefathers as well as exhibits on the Pilgrim story, Abolitionists, the Family and the American Covenant.

Visit www.thejenney.org for more information.

PUBLISHER NOTE

Generally Publisher Notes belong at the beginning of a book, however in this case I really wanted to save this for the back of the book, it had to be said after the *teaching* by Leo was complete.

In the fall of 2004, when I first saw what many have called "the best kept secret in America" I personally fell in love with the *Monument to the Forefathers*. That amazing edifice embodies all that is good in the American system and enshrines what has made us a great nation. Not just a great nation, but a *good* nation.

I often fear that the worn-out condition of the monument and the untended grounds around it are symbolic of the symptomatic ills of this nation as well. To the extent we as a people have disregarded the values enshrined in her visage, our nation and her once-venerated institutions have similarly suffered the ravages of time, unaided and worn down.

It is my sincere hope that this book will, in some small way, serve as a beacon of light directing attention to the principles of our founding and the importance of turning not to politicians and more government programs, but rather to God, the true source of all blessings to solve the problems that plague this and every nation.

The monument has within its hewn granite façade the keys of freedom, the source of real liberty, the principles of peace and the means to pursue happiness. Every generation that will study, learn and adhere to those principles will be thus blessed.

Boyd J. Tuttle

Publisher
Legends Library Publishing, Inc.
New York